ABT

⟦DK⟧ READERS

Level 3

Spacebusters: The Race to the Moon
Beastly Tales
Shark Attack!
Titanic
Aladdin
Heidi
Invaders from Outer Space
Plants Bite Back!
Time Traveler
Bermuda Triangle
Tiger Tales
Spies
Zeppelin
Terror on the Amazon
Disasters at Sea
The Story of Anne Frank
Movie Magic

Abraham Lincoln: Lawyer,
  Leader, Legend
George Washington: Soldier,
  Hero, President
Extreme Sports
Spiders' Secrets
LEGO: Mission to the Arctic
NFL: Super Bowl Heroes
MLB: Home Run Heroes: Big
  Mac, Sammy, and Junior
MLB: Roberto Clemente
MLB: Roberto Clemente (en español)
MLB: World Series Heroes
MLB: Record Breakers
The Big Dinosaur Dig
Space Heroes: Amazing Astronauts

Level 4

Antarctic Adventure
Days of the Knights
Volcanoes
Secrets of the Mummies
Pirates: Raiders of the High Seas
Horse Heroes
Micro Monsters
Extreme Machines
Flying Ace: The Story of
  Amelia Earhart
Free at Last! The Story of Martin
  Luther King, Jr.
First Flight: The Story of the Wright
  Brothers
The Incredible Hulk's Book
  of Strength
The Story of the Incredible Hulk
MLB: The Story of the New York
  Yankees
MLB: Strikeout Kings
MLB: Super Shortstops
MLB: The World of Baseball
JLA: Batman's Guide to Crime
  and Detection

JLA: Superman's Guide to
  the Universe
NFL's Greatest Upsets
NFL: Rumbling Running Backs
LEGO: Race for Survival
Going for Gold!
Atlantis: The Lost City
Black Beauty
Creating the X-Men
Crime Busters
Danger on the Mountain
D-Day Landings: The Story
  of the Allied Invasion
Dinosaur Detectives
Joan of Arc
Robin Hood
Space Station: Accident on Mir
Spider-Man's Amazing Powers
Spooky Spinechillers
The Story of Muhammed Ali
The Story of Spider-Man
The Story of the X-Men
Trojan Horse
Welcome to the Globe!

A Note to Parents and Teachers

DK READERS is a compelling program for beginning readers, designed in conjunction with leading literacy experts, including Dr. Linda Gambrell, director of the Eugene T. Moore School of Education at Clemson University. Dr. Gambrell has served on the Board of Directors of the International Reading Association and as president of the National Reading Conference.

Beautiful illustrations and superb full-color photographs combine with engaging, easy-to-read stories to offer a fresh approach to each subject in the series. Each DK READER is guaranteed to capture a child's interest while developing his or her reading skills, general knowledge, and love of reading.

The five levels of DK READERS are aimed at different reading abilities, enabling you to choose the books that are exactly right for your children:

Pre-Level 1 – Learning to read
Level 1 – Beginning to read
Level 2 – Beginning to read alone
Level 3 – Reading alone
Level 4 – Proficient readers

The "normal" age at which a child begins to read can be anywhere from three to eight years old, so these levels are only a general guideline.

No matter which level you select, you can be sure that you are helping your child learn to read, then read to learn!

LONDON, NEW YORK, MELBOURNE,
MUNICH, AND DELHI

Senior Editor Beth Sutinis
Editor Elizabeth Hester
Designer Tai Blanche
Assistant Managing Art Editor Michelle Baxter
Jacket Art Director Dirk Kaufman
DTP Designer Milos Orlovic
Production Chris Avgherinos

Reading Consultant
Linda Gambrell, Ph.D.

Produced by
Shoreline Publishing Group LLC
Editorial Director James Buckley, Jr.
Art Director Tom Carling
Carling Design, Inc.

Produced in partnership and licensed by
Major League Baseball Properties, Inc.
**Senior Vice President of Publishing
and MLB Photos** Don Hintze

First American Edition, 2004
04 05 06 07 08 10 9 8 7 6 5 4 3 2 1
Published in the United States by DK Publishing, Inc.
375 Hudson St., New York, NY 10014

Copyright © 2004 Dorling Kindersley Publishing, Inc.

All rights reserved under International and Pan-American Copyright
Conventions. No part of this publication may be reproduced, stored
in a retrieval system, or transmitted in any form or by any means, electronic,
mechanical, photocopying, recording, or otherwise, without the prior
written permission of the copyright owner.
Published in Great Britain by Dorling Kindersley Limited.

A catalog record for this book is available from the Library of Congress.
ISBN: 0-7566-0838-4 (PB)
0-7566-0837-6 (HC)

Color reproduction by Colourscan, Singapore

Printed and bound in China by L Rex Printing Co., Ltd.

Photography credits:
AP/Wide World: 5, 6, 38, 40, 41, 42; DK Photo Library: 45;
Corbis: 14, 15, 16, 19, 20, 23, 24, 27, 28, 31, 32, 36, 43, 45;
Getty Images: 35; Hulton Archive: 10.

Discover more at
www.dk.com

Contents

READERS

READING
3
ALONE

MAJOR LEAGUE BASEBALL™

DOWN TO
THE WIRE

Written by Michael Teitelbaum

DK Publishing, Inc.

Pennant race!

Every Major League Baseball team wants to reach the World Series and play for the championship of baseball. But first, they have to win the "pennant." Winning the pennant means that you are the champion of either the American League (A.L.) or the National League (N.L.). The battles to capture those league championships are called pennant races.

Sometimes the winner is not decided until the last game of the season.

Raise the flag

A pennant is a triangle-shaped flag. When a team wins the World Series, they get to raise the world championship pennant at their home stadium on Opening Day the following season. It is a thrilling moment for a team and its fans.

Cubs fans celebrated their team's pennant win in 2003.

A few times in baseball history, it has taken extra games to see who captures the pennant. During some seasons several teams stay in the pennant race right until the end. These races are the most exciting for fans.

The A.L. was formed in 1901 to join the N.L., which began in 1876. Until 1969, there was one pennant for each of those two leagues. The team with the best record in each league at the end of the regular season won the pennant.

In 1969, the leagues were split into two divisions, East and West. The teams with the best records in each division met in the League Championship Series (LCS) to determine the pennant winner.

In 1995, a Central Division was added to each league. The Division Series now determines which teams play in the LCS.

The Red Sox rejoiced after winning the A.L. East in 2003.

Now it takes 162 games plus two
playoffs to determine the league champs.
Read on for stories
of the most exciting
races in history!

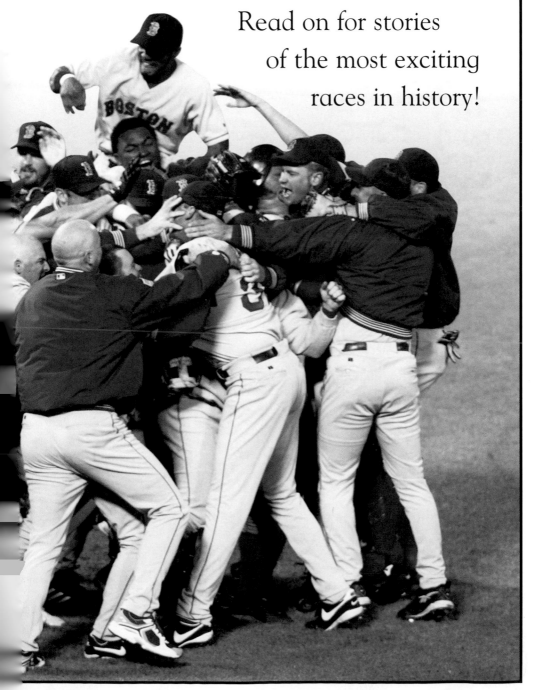

1908: The Merkle Mistake

By late September of 1908 the New York Giants and the Chicago Cubs were locked in a tight race for the N.L. pennant. When the teams met at New York's Polo Grounds on September 23, they were tied for first place.

The game was tied 1–1, going into the bottom of the ninth inning.

In the last of the ninth, the Giants had Moose McCormick on third and Fred Merkle on first with two outs.

Fred Merkle

Al Bridwell hit a single to center field. McCormick came home from third with the winning run. Game over, right? Wrong!

A mob of celebrating fans ran onto the field. Instead of touching second base, Merkle ran toward the clubhouse in centerfield. He thought the game was over.

An overflow crowd watches a Giants game in 1908.

9

Johnny Evers

The rules say that a player must touch the base safely or he can be called out. Johnny Evers of the Cubs saw this. He screamed for the ball. Giants fans and Cubs players fought for it on the crowded field.

Seeing this, Merkle tried to return through the screaming crowd to second base. The ball arrived first, and Merkle was called out. That meant that the run did not really score on the play.

The game could not continue because of the fans crowding the field. The umpires declared a tie.

None of this would have mattered if one of the teams finished the season ahead of the other. But both teams ended the season with identical 98–55–1 records.

On October 8, the tie game was replayed at the Polo Grounds. The Cubs won 4–2 to clinch the pennant. To this day, Merkle's baserunning mistake is one of the most famous foul-ups in baseball history.

MATHEWSON, N. Y. NAT'L

Giants Hall of Fame pitcher Christy Mathewson was the losing pitcher in the playoff.

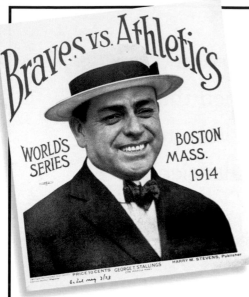

George Stallings

1914: Miracle Braves

In 1913, the Boston Braves finished 31½ games behind the pennant-winning New York Giants in the N.L. So when new Braves manager George Stallings took over the team for the 1914 season he didn't have high hopes.

As Stallings put it, "This club is a baseball horror."

The 1914 season started as most baseball fans expected. By July 4, the Giants were in first place. It looked like they were on their way to their fourth straight pennant. The Braves were in last place, 15 games out of first.

Then something amazing happened.
The Braves started winning.

Johnny Evers, who had come over
from the Cubs, began hitting and
playing great defense.
Three pitchers—
Bill James, Dick
Rudolph, and
Lefty Tyler—
started
winning
on a
regular basis.

*Catcher Hank
Gowdy was
another key part
of the 1914
Miracle Braves.*

Charlie Deal shows the Braves' all-black uniforms.

On July 19, the Braves finally
climbed out of the cellar (last place).
They started August with a nine-game
winning streak. On August 12, the
Braves reached second place. They
were quickly closing in on the Giants!

Then on September 8, the Boston Braves moved into first place. But they didn't stop there. The "Miracle Braves" captured the N.L. pennant, completing the greatest comeback ever.

In the World Series the Braves faced the Philadelphia Athletics, led by manager Connie Mack. Philadelphia was expected to win. But someone forgot to tell that to Boston!

The Braves completed their miracle season by sweeping the A's.

Connie Mack

Connie Mack was the owner and manager of the Philadelphia Athletics for 50 years (1901–1950). He won nine N.L. pennants and five World Series. He holds the record among all Major League managers for most games (7,878), most wins (3,776), and most losses (4,025).

1951: The shot heard 'round the world

The rivalry between the Brooklyn Dodgers and the New York Giants was one of the most intense in baseball history. In 1950, the Dodgers were coming off of

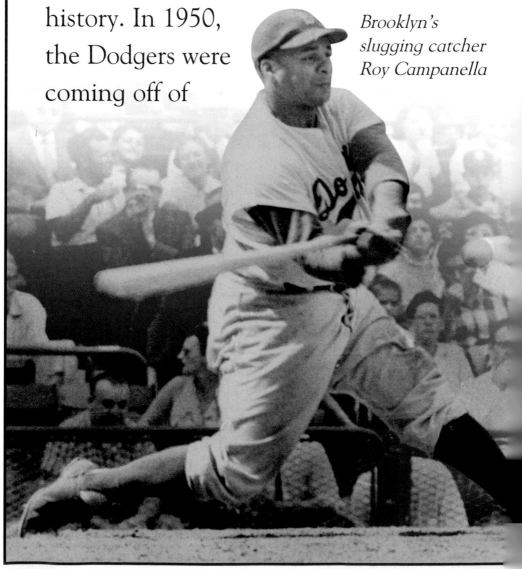

Brooklyn's slugging catcher Roy Campanella

a season that had broken their fans' hearts. They had lost the pennant to the Philadelphia Phillies on the season's final day.

By July of 1951, however, the Dodgers, led by catcher Roy

Willie Mays

Campanella, had opened up a $7\frac{1}{2}$ game lead over the second place Giants. By August, their lead was $13\frac{1}{2}$ games. In Brooklyn, the pennant seemed like a sure thing!

Then the Giants ran off a 16-game winning streak. The gap started to close. Led by rookie Willie Mays, the Giants won 39 of their last 47 games. The two teams ended the season *tied* for first place.

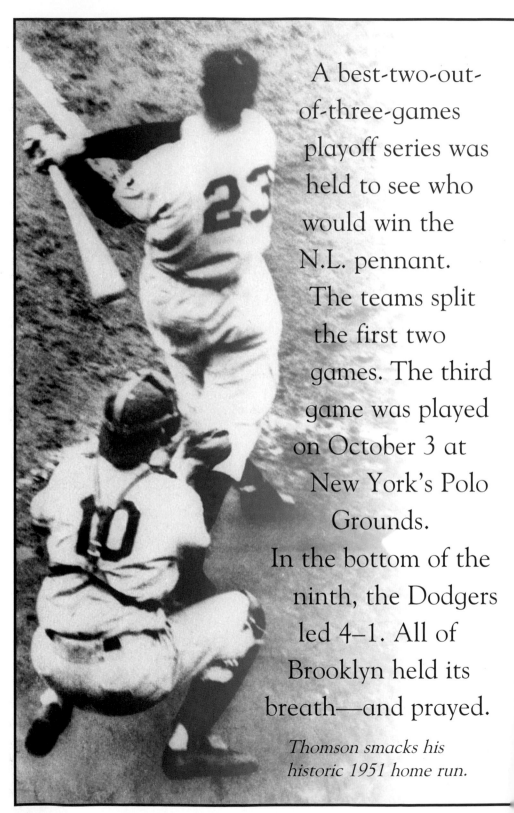

A best-two-out-of-three-games playoff series was held to see who would win the N.L. pennant. The teams split the first two games. The third game was played on October 3 at New York's Polo Grounds. In the bottom of the ninth, the Dodgers led 4–1. All of Brooklyn held its breath—and prayed.

Thomson smacks his historic 1951 home run.

The Giants scored to make it 4–2. They had two men on base. The Dodgers brought in Ralph Branca to pitch to Bobby Thomson.

Thomson smacked the second pitch into the left-field stands for a three-run, game-winning, pennant-clinching homer!

Russ Hodges, the Giants radio announcer screamed over and over "The Giants win the pennant!" The home run would become known as "The Shot Heard 'Round the World."

Hearts in Brooklyn were broken once again.

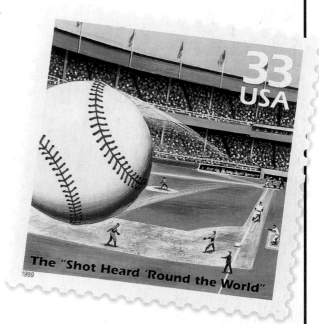

A stamp honors the homer.

1967: Boston's impossible dream

Some people called the 1967 American League pennant chase "The Great Race." Loyal and long-suffering fans of the Boston Red Sox called it "The Impossible Dream."

Denny McLain led the Tigers pitching staff in 1967.

The Red Sox had not won a pennant since 1946. They were not expected to win in 1967 as the season began.

Minnesota's Harmon Killebrew

The battle for the A.L. pennant raged into the final week of the season. Four teams were still in the race. The Detroit Tigers were a strong all-around team. The Chicago White Sox were nicknamed the "hitless wonders." No one on the White Sox hit above .250. They hung in using pitching, defense, and sheer willpower. After a change of managers, the Minnesota Twins came to life in July and joined the chase.

Jim Lonborg

The fourth team was the Red Sox. Boston had finished ninth in 1966. As they fought for the pennant in 1967, the Red Sox became the darlings of fans everywhere. Pitcher Jim Lonborg won an A.L.-best 22 games and struck out 246 batters.

Yaz's lefthanded swing was perfect for Boston's Fenway Park.

But the major force in Boston's run for the pennant was left fielder Carl Yastrzemski.

"Yaz" led the club on offense and defense. A great outfielder, he starred at the plate, too, leading the league with a .326 batting average and 121 RBI. He tied for the lead with 44 homers, too.

Finally, Chicago dropped out of the race. Heading into the final weekend, Minnesota led Boston and Detroit by one game. The Tigers had two doubleheaders that weekend, while the Twins had two games against Boston.

On Sunday, October 1, the final day of the 1967 season, Jim Lonborg won a 5–3 decision over the Twins, knocking Minnesota from the race.

Detroit won the first game of their doubleheader. If they won the second

Triple Crown

When a player leads his league in batting average, home runs, and RBI all in the same season, he is said to win the Triple Crown. In 1967, Boston's Carl Yastrzemski was the last Major League player to achieve this feat.

The Red Sox celebrate Lonborg's big win over the Twins.

game, they would finish the season in a tie with Boston. They lost and the Red Sox clinched the A.L. pennant. Boston's "Impossible Dream" had come true.

1978: Bucky's blast

In 1978, two longtime rivals—the Yankees and Red Sox—battled in one of baseball's most dramatic pennant races. By mid-season, fans were calling the Red Sox one of baseball's all-time great teams. Led by the hitting of Jim Rice, Fred Lynn,

Jim Rice

Carl Yastrzemski, and Carlton Fisk, and the pitching of Dennis Eckersley, Mike Torrez, and Luis Tiant, Boston dominated the A.L.

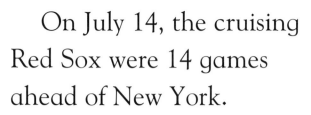

*Ron
Guidry*

On July 14, the cruising
Red Sox were 14 games
ahead of New York.

The defending
World Series–
champion
Yankees were
getting some great pitching, too. Starter
Ron Guidry would go 25–3 and win the
American League Cy Young Award.
Ace reliever Rich "Goose" Gossage
anchored the bullpen, winning 10 games
and saving 27 more.

But injuries to the rest of pitching
staff hurt the team. Despite having
hitting stars such as slugger Reggie
Jackson, outfielder Lou Piniella, and
catcher Thurman Munson, the
Yankees' offense struggled.

In mid-July, with the Yankees struggling, scrappy manager Billy Martin was fired. When Bob Lemon took over as Yankee manager on July 24, New York was $10\frac{1}{2}$ games behind Boston. Under the easygoing Lemon, the Yankees began winning. Guidry continued to pitch brilliantly, joined by Jim "Catfish" Hunter.

Meanwhile, Boston's lead began to shrink. On September 7, the Yankees traveled to Fenway Park for a key four-game series. The Red Sox had lost five of their last seven games, while the Yankees had won 12 of their last 14. Boston's lead had narrowed to only four games.

"Catfish" Hunter

Reggie Jackson

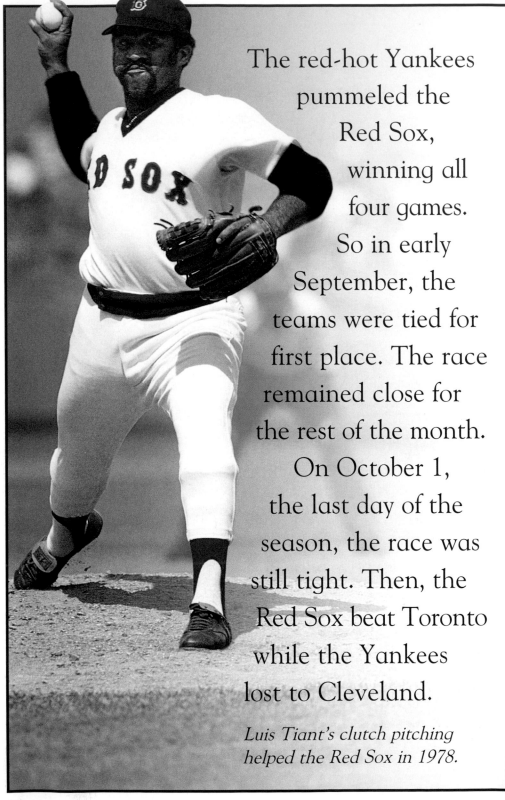

The red-hot Yankees pummeled the Red Sox, winning all four games. So in early September, the teams were tied for first place. The race remained close for the rest of the month. On October 1, the last day of the season, the race was still tight. Then, the Red Sox beat Toronto while the Yankees lost to Cleveland.

Luis Tiant's clutch pitching helped the Red Sox in 1978.

Amazingly, that meant that the two teams ended the regular season in a tie.

A one-game playoff was held on October 2 before a full house at Fenway Park. The entire season came down to this game. The winner would claim the A.L. East title.

Behind strong pitching by Mike Torrez, the Red Sox led 2–0 in the seventh inning.

Torrez had held the big Yankee bats in check. Then, with two outs and two men on in the seventh, Bucky Dent came to the plate. What happened next still makes Sox fans cry.

Mike Torrez

Bucky Dent touches home after his dramatic homer.

Dent had hit only four home runs that year, and would have just 22 over his six-year Major League career.

On the third pitch from Torrez, Dent stunned the Red Sox and their fans by lifting the ball high up into the "Green

Monster," a huge wall in left field, for a home run. The Yankees grabbed a 3–2 lead. They would go on to win the game 5–4 and with it, the A.L. East title.

The Yankees then beat the Kansas City Royals for the A.L. pennant. In the World Series, they completed their comeback, beating the Los Angeles Dodgers in six games.

But Red Sox fans will never forget the homer that smashed their pennant dreams in 1978.

Blaming the Babe

The Red Sox last won the World Series in 1918. In 1919, they sold Babe Ruth, also called "The Bambino" (Italian for "baby") to the Yankees. The Yankees flourished, but the Red Sox have not won a World Series since. Red Sox fans trace their bad luck to the "Curse of the Bambino."

1993: The final pitch

The 1993 pennant races were exciting in all four divisions.

In the N.L. East, the Phillies jumped out to a big lead. Then, in September, the Montreal Expos ran off a long winning streak, closing in on Philadelphia. The Phillies hung on and captured the division title by three games over the Expos.

The race in the N.L. West was a nail-biter all season long. The Atlanta Braves were expected to run away with the title behind their great pitchers, including Greg Maddux and Tom Glavine.

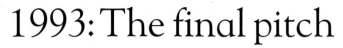

Greg Maddox

But the San Francisco Giants picked up slugger Barry Bonds.
In July, the Giants led the Braves by 10

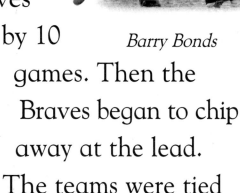

Barry Bonds

games. Then the Braves began to chip away at the lead. The teams were tied going into the final day of the season. Atlanta won its 104th game that day. The Giants lost to their longtime rivals, the Dodgers, to finish the season with only 103 wins.

Meanwhile, in the A.L. East, five teams battled through the season. Detroit, Boston, Baltimore, and the Yankees all stayed close to the Toronto Blue Jays. The Blue Jays finally climbed into first place, finishing seven games ahead of the second-place Yankees.

In the A.L. West, the Chicago White Sox, led by pitcher Jack McDowell and slugger Frank Thomas, battled the Texas Rangers. Riding the excitement of pitcher Nolan Ryan's final season, the Rangers came close, but then faded away, finishing eight games behind the White Sox.

Jack McDowell

In the
World Series,
Toronto met
Philadelphia to
create one of the
most exciting finishes
in baseball history.

Leading the series
three games to two, the
Blue Jays trailed 6–5 in
the bottom of the ninth
of Game 6. With two
men on base, Toronto's
Joe Carter lined a
three-run homer to
give Toronto the
championship
on the final pitch
of the season.

Joe Carter celebrates his Series-winning homer.

2003: Year of the curses

The Boston Red Sox have not won a World Series since 1918. The Chicago Cubs have not won the Series since 1908. Yet for all that time, no teams in Major League Baseball have had more loyal and devoted fans.

Yes, those letters are backward. Can you read them?

Both teams also have a "curse" in their histories, which some blame for their lack of postseason success. For a moment in October of 2003, it looked as if the two teams that have gone the longest without winning a World Series were going to meet in that year's Fall

Classic. It didn't quite turn out that way.

The 2003 race for division titles and wild-card spots came down to the last few days of the regular season. Then the playoffs started and things really heated up. The Yankees beat Minnesota in a Division Series to advance to the ALCS.

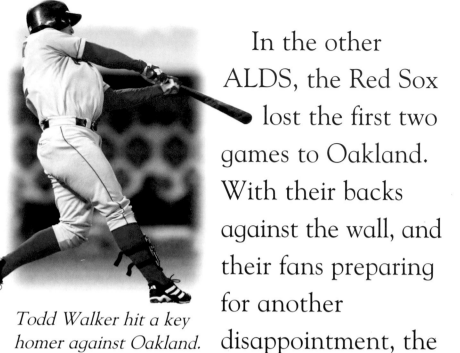

Todd Walker hit a key homer against Oakland.

In the other ALDS, the Red Sox lost the first two games to Oakland. With their backs against the wall, and their fans preparing for another disappointment, the Red Sox charged back. They won the final three games of the series, led by pitcher Pedro Martinez and slugger Manny Ramirez. They would now meet their archrivals, the Yankees, in the ALCS to decide the league pennant.

In the N.L., the Florida Marlins began their own

Kerry Wood

"Cinderella story" run for the championship by beating the San Francisco Giants in four games. The Chicago Cubs, meanwhile, battled the Atlanta Braves in a back-and-forth five-game series. The Cubs won the first game, then the teams alternated victories until Chicago won the Series behind the strong pitching of Kerry Wood in Game 5. The much-loved Cubs and Marlins met in the NLCS.

A Cubs' victory was just out of reach.

Both League Championship Series captured baseball fans' imaginations. After four games, the Cubs were only one win away from their first trip to the Fall Classic since 1945. But with ace Josh Beckett pitching, Florida won Game 5 for the Marlins.

With one out in the eighth inning of Game 6 at Wrigley Field in Chicago, the Cubs led 3–0. Just five outs to go!

But a fan knocked a foul ball out of the reach of Chicago's Moises Alou. The play kept the Marlins' rally alive. As Chicago's fans watched in silence, the Marlins stormed ahead to win 8–3.

In the Game 7, Marlins rookie Miguel Cabrera drove in four runs, sending the Marlins to the World Series. The 59-year-old "Goat Curse" lived on.

Florida's Ugueth Urbina and Ivan Rodriguez

In the ALCS, the Yankees and Red Sox battled a dramatic seventh game. The Red Sox needed one more win to finally advance to the World Series.

With one out in the eighth inning of Game 7, Boston led 5–2. Like the Cubs, they had just five outs to go! Pedro Martinez seemed to be

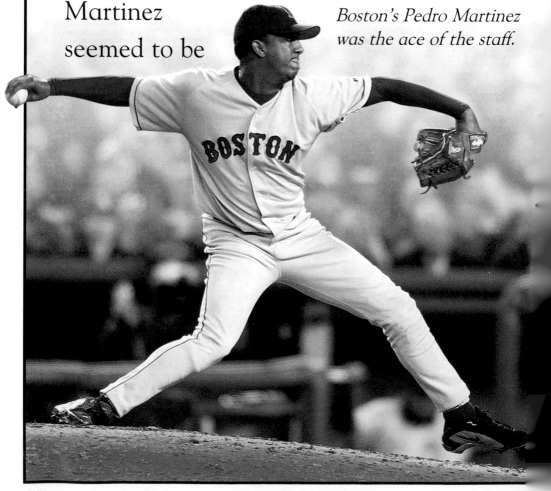

Boston's Pedro Martinez was the ace of the staff.

in control. But then the Yankees struck quickly, tying the game. Finally, Aaron Boone led off the bottom of the 11th inning with a home run that sent the Yankees to the World Series.

Aaron Boone

Red Sox fans once again muttered about the "Curse of the Bambino" (see page 33). And the world was left to wonder what a Cubs–Red Sox World Series might have been like.

The Goat Curse

"Billy Goat" Sianis, a Chicago restaurant owner, and his goat were denied entrance to Wrigley Field for the 1945 World Series. Angry and upset, Sianis put the "Goat Curse" on the team. The Cubs lost that Series and have not been back since.

The Major Leagues

American League (founded 1901)

A.L. East Division
Baltimore Orioles
Boston Red Sox
New York Yankees
Tampa Bay Devil Rays
Toronto Blue Jays

A.L. Central Division
Chicago White Sox
Cleveland Indians
Detroit Tigers
Kansas City Royals
Minnesota Twins

A.L. West Division
Anaheim Angels
Oakland Athletics
Seattle Mariners
Texas Rangers

National League (founded 1876)

N.L. East Division
Atlanta Braves
Florida Marlins
Montreal Expos
New York Mets
Philadelphia Phillies

N.L. Central Division
Chicago Cubs
Cincinnati Reds
Houston Astros
Milwaukee Brewers
Pittsburgh Pirates
St. Louis Cardinals

N.L. West Division
Arizona Diamondbacks
Colorado Rockies
Los Angeles Dodgers
San Diego Padres
San Francisco Giants

Glossary

American League (A.L.)
One of two groups of teams that make up the Major Leagues

cellar
Last place in a league or division

Cinderella team
A team that is not expected to do well, but surprises everyone by winning

Cy Young Award
Named for a famous pitcher, this award is given every year to the top pitcher in each league.

doubleheader
Two games played on the same day between the same two teams

Fall Classic
A nickname for the World Series, which is almost always played in October

National League (N.L.)
One of two groups of teams that make up the Major Leagues

pennant
A triangle-shaped flag; also the name of the championship of each of the two Major Leagues

playoffs
A series of games played after the regular season to determine the championship

postseason
The period of time during which a series of games is played after the regular season to determine the championship

rivalry
Intense competition

slugger
A batter who hits with great power and usually hits lots of home runs

split
When two teams play two games, and each team wins one of the games

sweep
To win all the games in a series without losing

Triple Crown
An unofficial award given to a hitter who leads his league in home runs, RBI, and batting average all in the same season